Visual

Vocab

Other books by Donna McGeorge

The Pen is Mightier than the Slide (2014)

Get Engaged (2015)

Visual

Vocab

200 Words

800 Pictures

Compiled and drawn

by Donna McGeorge

First published in 2015

National Library of Australia Cataloguing-in-Publication entry:

Author:	Donna McGeorge 1966 –
Title:	Visual Vocab Vol 1: 200 Words 800 Pictures
ISBN:	978-1-326-32063-8
Subjects:	Training
	Presenting
	Drawing
	Visual Thinking
	Communication

Illustrations and layout: Donna McGeorge
Cover design: Donna McGeorge

To all my friends and colleagues who work in the visual field.

I have learned so much since finding this tribe of insightful, visionary and talented people.

Visual Vocab - 5

6 - Visual Vocab

Contents

8 – Visual Vocab

About this book

People often ask me if I have always been artistic. My typical response was always no, until I remembered that my mother has been an artist all her life, and that I did quite well in all my artistic pursuits at school.

I don't think of myself as artistic though. I think of myself as someone who can think in pictures, and translate words into visuals and yet I don't ever describe myself as a "visual person" or "visual learner".

I think it's all about using lines and shapes cleverly ... and being resourceful. I know where and how to find pictures.

So, what I have compiled here is a visual dictionary of sorts that contains words I frequently have heard in my business and corporate travels along with four ways to represent these concepts visually.

I do not consider myself the creator of these images, but more the *curator* of them. Many come from my imagination, and some have been collected from watching others, my library of visual books, Google images, symbols and iconography.

I have titled it Volume I because no doubt there will be words I have missed that deserve to be in a second volume.

These pictures are neither perfect nor complete. They are also my interpretation of meaning. I encourage you to take these images, make them your own and make meaning for yourself.

I welcome suggestions, feedback, thoughts and examples of how you are using these pictures in your work. Please leave them at www.visualvocab.com.au.

Happy drawing!

Visual Vocab - 9

Visual

Vocab

Absent

Accomplish

Accountability

Achievement

Action

Affection

Alignment

Amazing

Ambiguous

Appreciate

Attitude

Attraction

Authority

Automate

Awareness

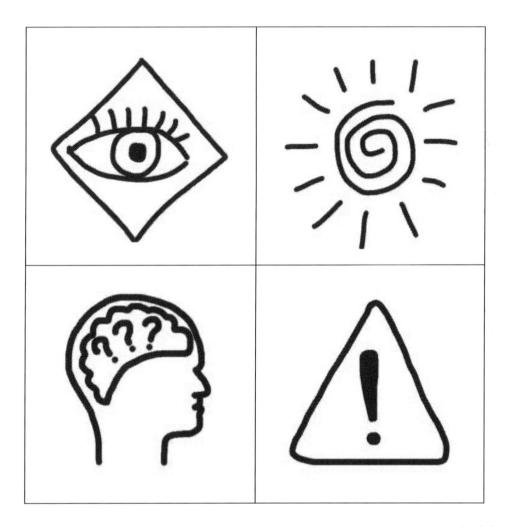

Awesome

Balance

Bargain

Benefit

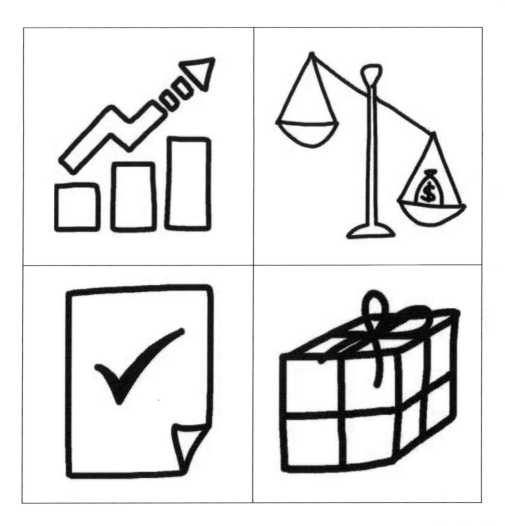

Brainstorm

Breakthrough

Broken

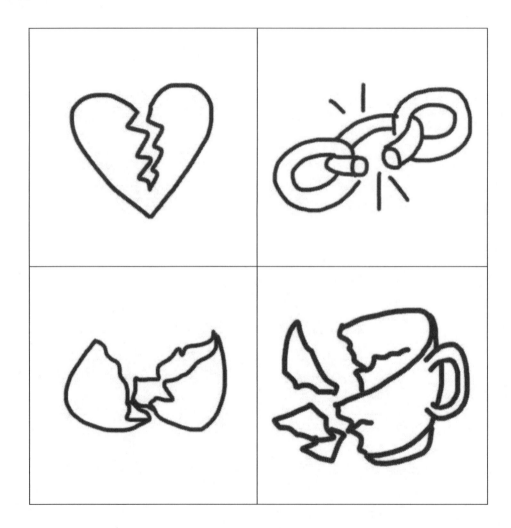

Budget

Building Blocks

Buildings

Business

Capacity

Caution

Celebrate

Certification

Change

Chaos

Choice

Circulate

Co-Create

Co-Operate

Coach

Collaborate

Communication

Community

Complexity

Conflict

Confusion

Connect

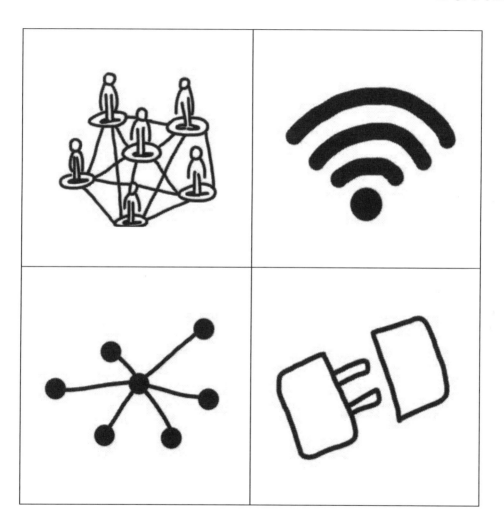

Consensus

Consulting

Contract

Control

Conventional

Correspondence

Create

Crisis

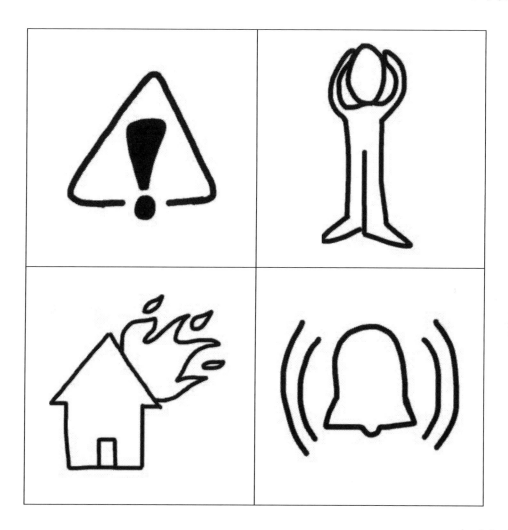

Curiosity

Customer

Danger

Data

Deadline

Deceive

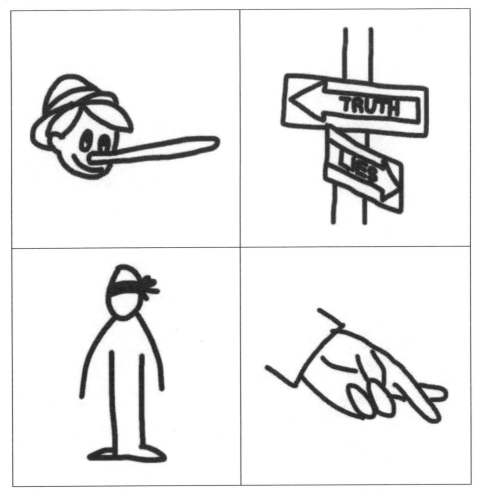

Define

Deliver

Demonstrate

Diagnose

Different

Direction

Disruption

Distribution

Diverge

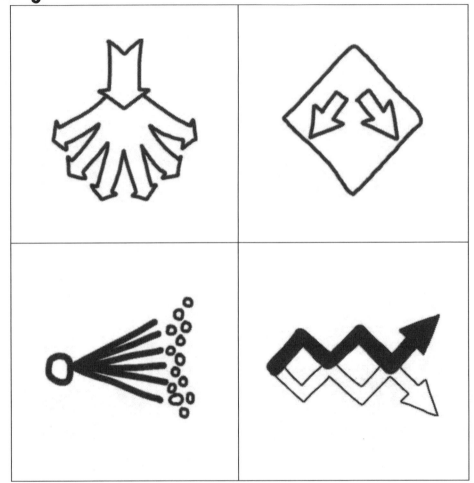

Diversity

Drama

Dream

Economy

Emphasise

Employ

Empowerment

Enable

Encourage

yes you CAN !

Energy

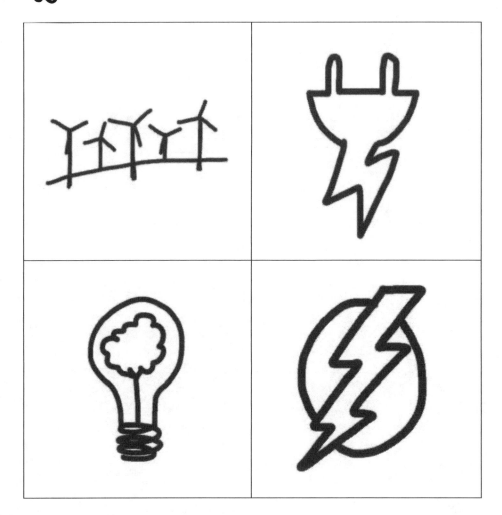

Equipment

Exercise

Explore

Face to Face

Fairness

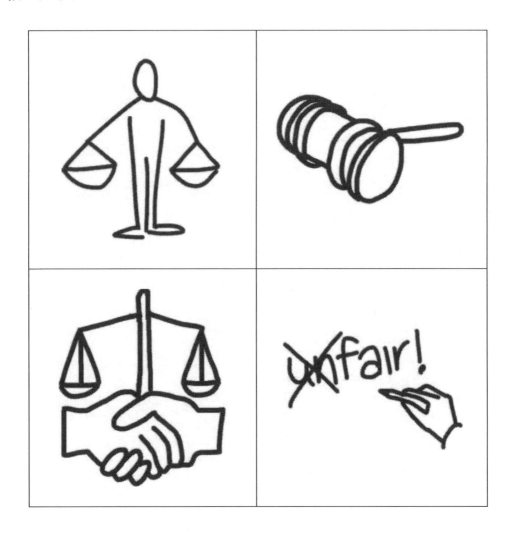

Family

Feedback

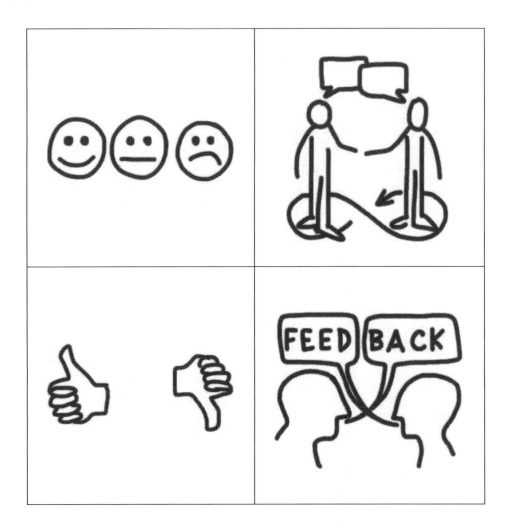

Finance

Flexible

Footprint

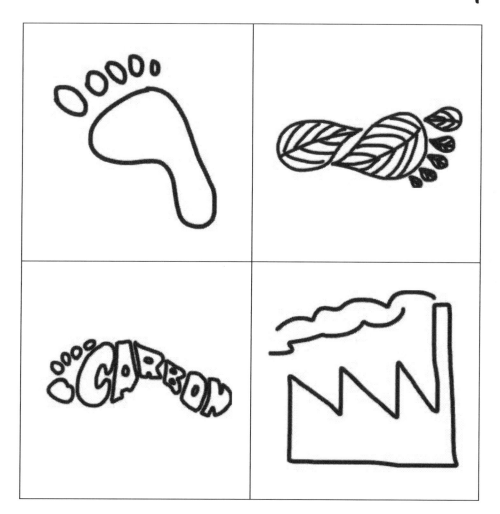

Forecast

Freedom

Frequency

Future

Game

Gap

Gender

Generate

Global

Government

Group

Growth

Harmony

Haste

History

Holistic

Horror

Idea

Identify

Ignore

Important

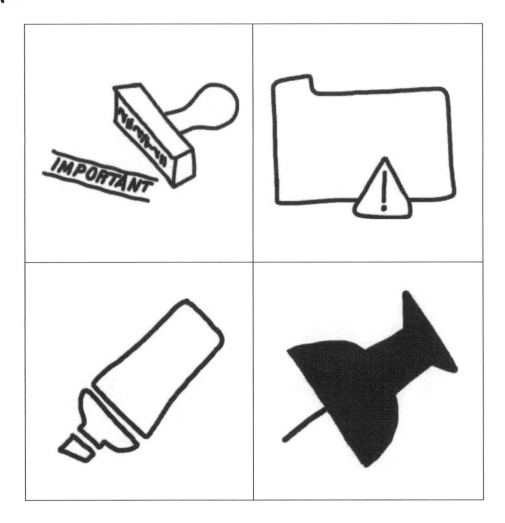

Improve

Inclusion

Inflation

Information

Inspiration

Insurance

Integration

Invention

Isolation

Jackpot

Join

Justice

Knowledge

Kudos

Label

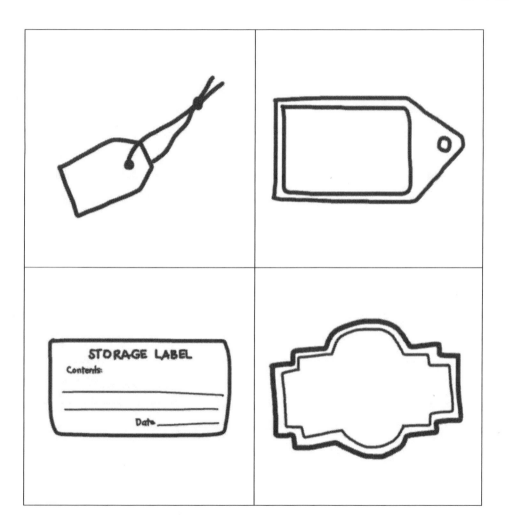

Within the illustration: STORAGE LABEL / Contents: / Date

Landmark

Leadership

Learn

Liability

Assets | Liabilities

Listen

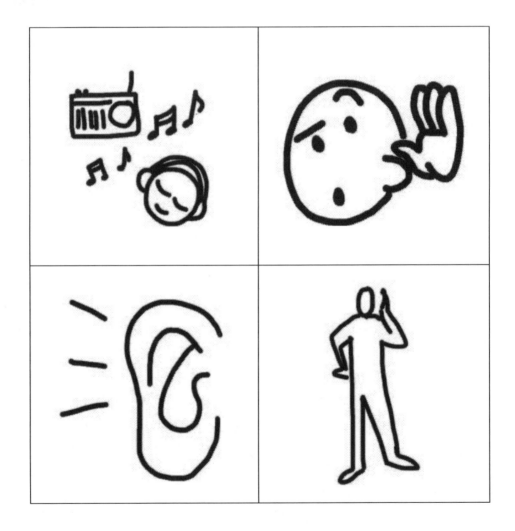

Logical

Love

Luck

Magic

Maintain

Manufacture

Market

Measure

Message

Momentum

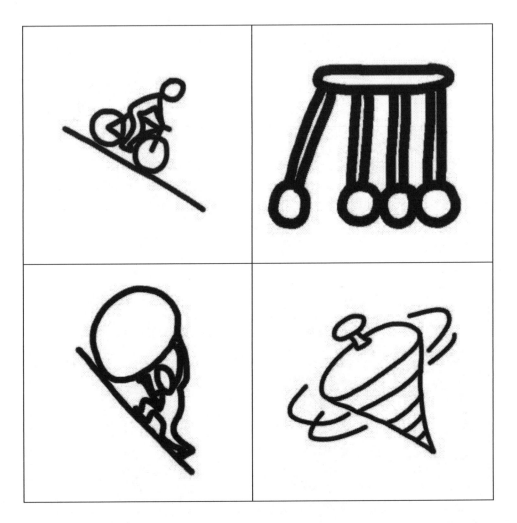

Motivate

Myth

Negotiate

Network

New

No

Objective

Obstacle

Occupation

Opportunity

Organise

Outsource

Partnership

Perspective

Plan

Pollution

Positive

Power

Premium

Presentation

Problem

Process

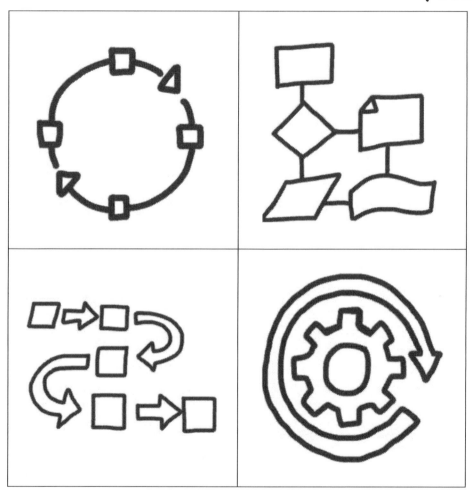

Progress

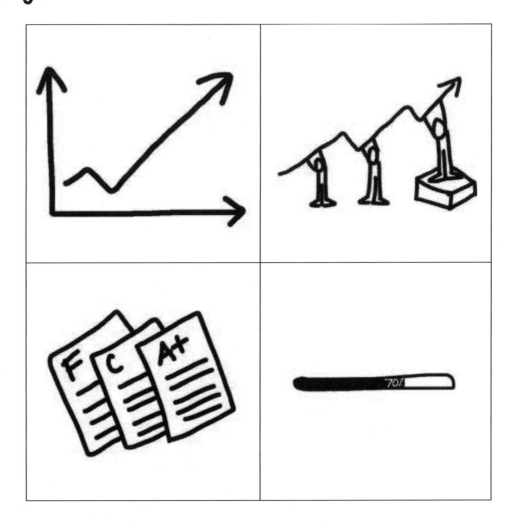

Protect

Purpose

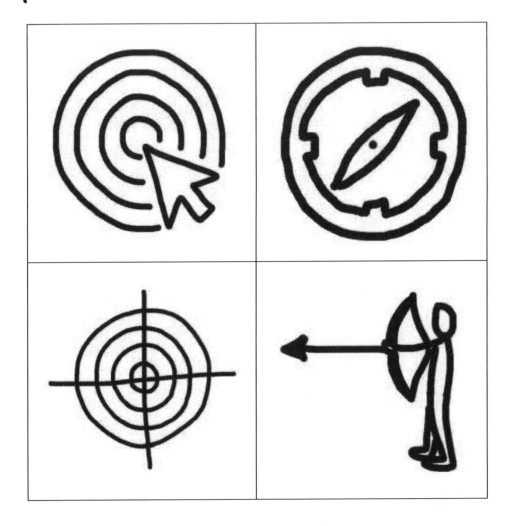

Recruitment

Relationship

Resilient

Safety

Schedule

Season

Speed

Story

Strength

Structure

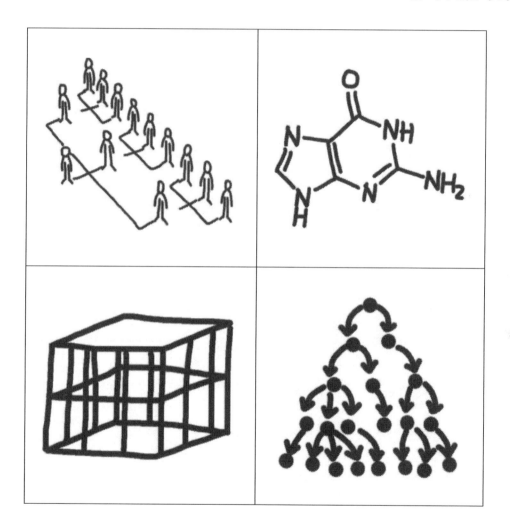

Success

Synergy

Team

Technology

Think

Toolkit

Training

Transformation

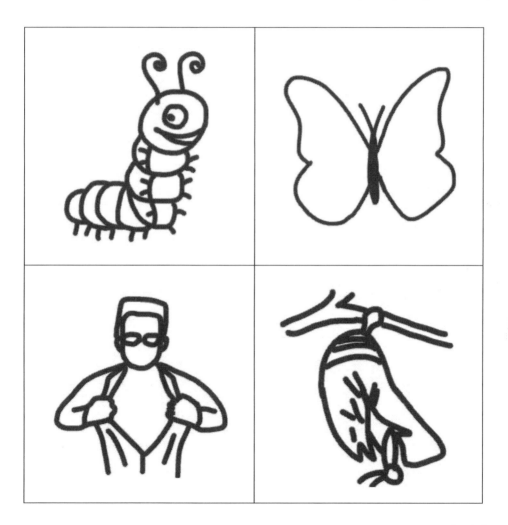

Transport

Travel

Trust

Understand

Values

Versatile

Victory

Virtual

Vision

Waste

Wealth

Welcome

You

Your

Visual

Vocab

Index

Index

Index

Index

Index

Index

Index

Index

Index

Index

Stay Tuned

for

Volume II

Made in the USA
Lexington, KY
08 February 2019